DAILY MOTIVATION
With the Number 1 Results Coach

This is Your Year

Volume One

By

Shawn Shewchuk

Results Press
Unit 229
#180, 8601 Lincoln Blvd.
Los Angeles, California
90045

www.theresultspress.com

ISBN: 978-1-953089-86-1

First Edition

Copyright © 2020 by Shawn Shewchuk

All rights reserved. No part of this book may be reproduced in any form without the prior writer permission from the publisher. The opinions and conclusions drawn in this book are solely those of the author. The author and publisher bear no liability in connection with the use of the ideas presented.

About SHAWN SHEWCHUK

Shawn Shewchuk is widely regarded as a leader in the area of achievement and performance and has skyrocketed to being one of the most sought-after speakers, coaches, and wealth-building authorities worldwide. Through his coaching, speaking, bestselling and ground-breaking methodologies, he has impacted the results of countless individuals and numerous organizations throughout North America and beyond.

Shawn Shewchuk is the direct link to the achievement of your objectives. The results experienced by those he has worked with have been so remarkable that he has become known as "The Number 1 Results Coach."

Shawn Shewchuk has founded numerous companies, including Change Your Results Inc., which is headquartered in Western Canada but operates globally.

Visit www.changeyourresults.com

DAILY MOTIVATION

With the Number 1 Results Coach

This is Your Year

Volume One

INTRODUCTION

When you have those moments, (and you and everyone else on this little planet have them), there are 4 points of application that keep you moving forward, notwithstanding whatever may have happened or may be happening.

The first is your refusal to give energy to whatever it is that is causing you to doubt your trajectory. You are human and are, therefore, more intelligent than any non-human on this little globe. You have been gifted with the ability to accept, reject, or ignore any thought or idea that comes to you from external sources or your own internal dialogue. If you must doubt something, doubt your fears.

The second is focus. Your attention, your execution of those predetermined actions, must continue. You are the sole source of the energy that is moving you forward, even in the face of challenges that may initially appear insurmountable. Ensure that you are focused on the outcomes that you want, need, desire, and deserve to the exclusion of all outside distractions. Your mental toughness is what you will employ to carry you through anything that life may throw your way.

The third is what you absorb. We aren't talking about sunlight, although that is good, we are talking about what you absorb from those you choose to surround yourself with. This is one of, if not the most, important pieces of advice you could be given. You will become exactly like those you associate with. Take the steps today to surround yourself with the people that force you to grow and challenge yourself, just by being around them. Never settle. Never be satisfied. If you're the smartest person in the room, you're in the wrong room.

The fourth and final of these points is what you feed yourself. No, not the food you eat three times a day but the knowledge you consciously choose to take in. This involves a few different activities that you need to engage in regularly, and there are absolutely no substitutes. You need to invest time reading daily; real books that you gain knowledge and awareness from, not fiction. You must attend events such as seminars, boot camps, and training at least four times a year. You need to have a coach that you invest in financially, not just a mentor.

Last but definitely not least, you need to journal every day.

Your life, relationships, and business or career will change exponentially within just 12 short months.

Choose to **live an inspired life.**

Welcome to your new life.

January

Paradigm Shift

"You can't break a habit; you have to replace it."
— Shawn Shewchuk

For the month of January, we are going to invest time on how you will achieve your goals and objectives through shifting your paradigms. Decide which habit you are going to shift. Determine the polar opposite of the one habit you want to change. Make an irrevocable decision every day in January to focus on and engage in the opposite of your current habit.

Within the month, you will have replaced your old habit.

JANUARY 1

Think about it. Is today a day of soon-to-be-forgotten New Year's resolutions? Or is today the day of real and meaningful change? That is the decision.

Decide now what you want next New Year's Day to look like for you, in all aspects of life.

It is your time to play big—to step up, take control of your direction, embrace and engage with what is rightfully yours. You deserve the best year that life has to offer. Now go and contribute to make that a reality.

Happy New Year to you!

JANUARY 2

I remember being seven years old, and it was New Year's Eve. My Dad shared something profound with me. At the time I, of course, did not realize how applicable it was. He said, "Shawn, while we celebrate the start of a new year, and we look forward to new beginnings, it is about so much more. Every day is a new beginning and an opportunity to start fresh, no matter how good or bad any prior day was."

Your destination or goal needs to be clear and defined. If you do not know or are unable to see where you are going, you will waste your life running in circles.

Spend the time today to set, define, and become clear about where you are going.

I promise you, you'll be grateful you did!

JANUARY 3

Life is about service.

It is through service that we raise one another higher and higher.

Always be of service.

JANUARY 4

If you already know how to do it, it is not a goal.

There is only one reason for a goal... GROWTH.

Your goals should be big.

Whatever your goal is, double it!

A goal should inspire, motivate, and scare you all at the same time. If it doesn't, it's not big enough.

JANUARY 5

Once you know where you are going with clarity about your destination, life becomes simpler.

What is your destination?

Give yourself permission and then create the most incredible destination that your imagination can conjure up.

Now go do something about it.

JANUARY 6

_____

The process of setting a goal will not ensure you achieve it.

There is no inspiration in needs; we all know how to acquire what we need. The inspiration is in knowing what we want and going after it.

Decide what you want, define it in detail, and then get after it. THINK BIG!

Double, triple, and quadruple your goal. It needs to scare the life out of you.

Spend more time achieving your goal and less time setting your goal.

JANUARY 7

You need to know and be extremely clear on the answer to this question. Do not waste time overthinking and overanalyzing. You already know what you want, so all you must do today is decide.

We talked about it yesterday. You have had a lot of time to think about it, and now you move. Today, at this very moment in time.

Go ahead, answer it.

WHAT DO YOU REALLY WANT?

JANUARY 8

In addition to your goals, you will need to do a little more. You need to lay out the predetermined action steps you are going to take.

Without these, you could get hung up on the **How**.

Now that you know and have established what you want, you need to reverse engineer it. Break it down by what you need to do every year, every month, every day, and, for some of us, every hour. Block time in your calendar to implement those action steps, those bite-sized pieces.

Execution of predetermined action steps is what you do on an hourly, daily, and monthly basis.

JANUARY 9

———————

Your goals and action steps need to be specific and quantified. In other words, do not say "I want more money." More is a relative term; you need to put a specific figure to your goal.

Now that you have done this, you should commit it to paper. Think with your pen.

Do it now!

JANUARY 10

Review your goals at least once a week.

In addition, set a few minutes aside every three months to revisit and, if necessary, update your goals.

This also acts as your Accountability Check Point (ACP). This gives you the all-important opportunity to determine your progress; to ensure that you are taking the action steps necessary to attain your grand goals.

You want to get there, right?

JANUARY 11

_____

Life is a gift and a game. Don't get too serious about it. Enjoy it!

Start playing!

JANUARY 12

If you need to augment or expand your goals or change direction for any reason, go ahead and do it. There is one thing that you want to avoid, and that is reducing your goals. Always keep increasing your goals.

Refuse to allow fear to dominate!

JANUARY 13

Smile today and every day. You'll be surprised at the difference it makes. Smiling improves your life as well as positively impacting those with whom you come into contact.

Your energy changes. Your outlook and perspective change. Your attitude and disposition change. All your interactions change. Your environment changes. Your business changes. Your career changes. All your relationships change.

ALL of these and many more changes are improvements! YOUR LIFE IMPROVES when you smile.

It can make the difference between just another day and a phenomenal day. You deserve to have phenomenal days every day.

JANUARY 14

You really want to achieve your goals. You are willing to do whatever it takes. You are taking the predetermined steps that you need to take, based on your BIG goals.

Always focus on what you want! Never focus on what you don't want.

Without exception, what you focus on you will receive and achieve.

JANUARY 15

Embrace your power, become engaged with your life, conduct yourself as you never have in the past. Take steps that you have hesitated about in the past and take real action right now.

You will be blown away by what you accomplish.

JANUARY 16

Spend time with those who are important to you. Spent time with those who lift you up, who support you, who encourage you and motivate you. Spend as much time as you can with like-minded and driven humans.

Avoid or limit the time you spend with those who are detractors; those who claim to support you but don't actually believe in you; whose actions are not aligned with what they profess and who say and do what is in their best interest—at your expense.

Those you spend the most time with dictate your success. You are who you associate with the most. There are no exceptions!

JANUARY 17

If you can't change it, give it absolutely no time or energy. Your time, energy, and money should be directed only at effecting positive change in all you do.

The past cannot be changed. Stop worrying and focusing on the events of the past. You can't change them, and worrying about unalterable outcomes will only serve to bring more of the same into your life.

Learn from past experiences and life-lessons, never dwell on the past, and expend no energy on anything from your past.

JANUARY 18

Your income is directly tied to your goals, paradigms, activity/time management, and work ethic; not the economy.

JANUARY 19

It's all in how you treat it. Money, that is.

No matter what you've been told or what you may have read, money is neither good nor bad. Money is simply a tool. Just for a moment, think about this: if you were a house framer and you showed up on a job site to frame a new house but refused to get out of your truck and utilize your tools, would you be any good as a framer? The overwhelming consensus is, no. Money is a tool and works the same way. You need to treat it as a tool. You need to acquire more of it if you want to achieve higher levels of freedom and help those who need help.

It's not about the money—it's about what money can do for you and others.

JANUARY 20

Your focus is a determinant of your outcomes. Always focus on abundance and prosperity. Never justify scarcity with an indication that money isn't important. The more you have, the more you can achieve. The more you have, the more you can help.

It's extremely difficult, perhaps even impossible, to make a positive impact without a positive cash flow.

JANUARY 21

Awareness is knowledge. The deeper your reservoir of knowledge, the more powerful you become.

Educate yourself. Dedicate time every day to bettering yourself. Study the material that benefits you in true progression. Attend events and seminars that inspire and challenge you; that focus on imparting a wealth of practical and useful knowledge. Hire a coach to be your sounding board and a guide to assist you and hold you accountable.

Utilize this immense wealth of information that you have and continue to acquire at every intersection and crossroad, to ensure that you are headed in the right direction.

JANUARY 22

Your life is made up of moments called "now."

Love your life to its fullest. Seek out and find amazing and life-changing opportunities and experiences. Become involved in activities that interest you and do those things that you've always wanted and planned to do someday... today.

Don't wait, don't find reasons why you can't, and don't justify inaction. We don't know and are unable to guarantee tomorrow.

If not now, when?

JANUARY 23

Anything!

That's what you can do.

You can do anything you want to.

Don't permit anything or anyone to be a stumbling block to your achieving anything you want to achieve. If you determine not to allow those stumbling blocks to be impediments and instead choose to view them as steppingstones, your progress will astound you.

JANUARY 24

Banish fear—it leaves more people stranded in conformity, mediocrity, and unhappiness than any other conditioned emotion.

And it doesn't exist outside of your mind.

JANUARY 25

You were placed on this planet for a reason. To leave this planet slightly better than when you arrived is an admirable objective.

This special purpose is something you may not even be aware of. It is something that only you were intended to carry out, a mission possible for you, something that will leave a lasting impact… A legacy.

What is your legacy going to be?

JANUARY 26

If you've ever wondered why some experience huge success while others don't, here's the answer.

Those that make it big refuse to permit fear to control them. They shut out detractors. They set massive goals; the kinds that make others question their sanity. They are 100% focused on what they want and know what they don't want; they invest time and energy only on what they really want. They take massive risks, and they know it. They have faith and are tenacious, and no matter how hard it gets or how difficult it may seem, they never give up or concede.

The missing component for most humans is that they don't execute. You as the high achiever—take action on those previously discussed predetermined steps.

High achievers are always moving forward. They execute their goals and action plans. They are accountable!

JANUARY 27

There is always a risk when we embrace change. You can't avoid risk, nor should you. But you should manage risk by making calculated decisions and not overanalyzing.

Face risk head-on and master the alignment between risk and reward. When you operate this way, the risk will recede or become much less relevant.

You know it's coming, so expect it.

JANUARY 28

Life is about other humans, your humans.

Make time today to let those you care about know that you care. Call them, text them, email them, go visit them today.

Tell them that you love them. Don't assume that they know.

JANUARY 29

Hesitation, avoidance, and over-analysis… all cause us disappointment, discouragement, and depression.

Resolve to "do it" and "start" today.

JANUARY 30

The two most powerful forces available to us are **love** and **gratitude**.

Live a life of deep and meaningful love in all areas, with an appreciation for all of life's awesome gifts.

Your lifestyle of gratitude opens the floodgates to immense and incalculable benefits.

Without reservation, live in an attitude of gratitude.

JANUARY 31

Start today...

Live from the inside out, not the outside in. Refuse to permit outside sources to impact and influence you, unless it's the influence you want and one that will contribute to attaining your goals.

Your high level of personal awareness is key over the societal norms and the binding effects of the masses.

Become inner-directed, not outer-directed.

February

Persistence

"Persistence is about a lack of so-called common sense. Traditional and prevailing societal norms would dictate that when it appears that the world is against you, throw in the towel and start over. But keep persisting. There are no do-overs in life."
– Shawn Shewchuk

For the month of February, we focus on sticking with your chosen path to achievement, even when you encounter those pesky stumbling blocks. Here is a little advice for you about those stumbling blocks: you need to use them as steppingstones. You will feel like giving up, and others may tell you that you're crazy for sticking with such a far-fetched idea. That's okay.

Some days, this will take everything you've got and then some. Override all emotional responses; refuse to listen to detractors or internalize distractions. This is a minute-by-minute decision.

FEBRUARY 1

Spend your life seeking out and finding opportunities. Most opportunities are missed. This is only because most people are focused on the problems rather than the opportunities that those problems present. The outcomes you have set for yourself are what is important; these manifest when you embrace what you desire and deserve.

Refuse to allow outside forces to control your viewpoint or resulting activities. Focus on solutions, opportunities, and how you can make a difference in the lives of others.

Life offers some amazing and rewarding opportunities. Take advantage of these today!

FEBRUARY 2

Unfortunately, there are enough people against you. Let that be their business. They don't know what you know. Be for you, not against you.

Make the decision to reach moment-by-moment decisions to stay on your own road of achievement.

You have the potential, ability, and power. Live life on your terms.

FEBRUARY 3

When things look their bleakest, remember the following: When you change, the world changes with you.

Make the changes you wish to see, today.

FEBRUARY 4

The time to start or do something will never be exactly right. Waiting, or failing to start for any reason, is only procrastination. Justifying the reasons for not starting will only prolong your misery.

The opposite of procrastination is accountability. Be accountable to yourself and your coach.

START!

FEBRUARY 5

When you speak from the heart, it's always authentic, always real, and always honest.

Before you speak, always be focused on how you can put the interests of others first.

FEBRUARY 6

Find a mentor; develop a relationship and ask for their advice.

Mentors will assist you in seeing possibilities and removing blinders. You will be able to see more clearly.

FEBRUARY 7

A big goal is imperative.

The following Law of 3's outlines the following 3 steps to achievement; these are as important in the achievement of the goal as setting the goal is.

-You must get crystal clear on your goal (the destination) with no ambiguity.
-You need to have a laser focus, to the exclusion of all outside distractions.
-You need to execute the action steps that you have previously laid out.

And, of course, you must be accountable. Burn these into your memory and refer to them often.

FEBRUARY 8

Your internal conversations have as much of an impact on you and your results as those you verbalize. Be always vigilant and aware of what you think, say, and internalize. This includes the internal battles that you wage with yourself.

Remove and extinguish disparaging thoughts and ideas. Never speak ill or negatively of another human being. What happens inside manifests itself on the outside.

Always maintain your focus in conversation (both internal and verbalized), thoughts, and actions on how you would prefer to be seen, discussed, and thought about.

Positive outcomes are always key!

FEBRUARY 9

Today is a gift and is full of gifts. Enjoy today and today's gifts.

There is only one true guarantee in this life: none of us are getting out of this alive. Life is terminal. ☺

Live to be the best, enjoy each gifted moment, be of service, and focus on ways to leave this world a better place than you found it.

FEBRUARY 10

Take a long, hard look inside. Decide who you are and determine how you got there.

Now for the all-important step: decide who you want to become.

Remember, what got you to where you are won't get you to where you want to go.

FEBRUARY 11

It takes no more energy to think big than it does to think small.

It's time to go from the kiddie pool into the deep end. Dive in and make a big splash.

Think of the best life you could possibly have and go for it. Think of the most rewarding and profitable business/career you could have and pursue it. Think of what the outcomes would be if you had the best and most powerful relationships possible; now go contribute to the growth of those relationships.

FEBRUARY 12

Today, focus on service. Service is about giving without the expectation of a return.

Bear in mind the value you bring and deliver. Be of service and never sell yourself short.

Put simply, life should be about service to others.

FEBRUARY 13

Change is your friend; uneasiness is your ally, and the new is for growth.

Embrace the above ideal; always be seeking to increase awareness and intentionally placing yourself in situations that ensure your upward motion and forward progress.

Remember, awareness is knowledge.

FEBRUARY 14

Love is one (of two) of the most powerful forces known and available to us on this planet. Embrace love, give and emanate love, and (most importantly) live your life in love.

Express love.

Celebrate love in all forms.

FEBRUARY 15

Find out what makes good days good. Once you know what makes good days good, insert more of that into your life and focus on always having great days!

Celebrate the good days. Then turn good days into great days!

FEBRUARY 16

The highest function we can perform is to think. This is what sets us apart from any other creature on the planet.

We have the gift of choice. To choose is to live the life that we design. Make your own decision today. It should include a "design your own life" component, as only you can make that reality.

Live by design, not by default.

FEBRUARY 17

When you are faced with what may appear as insurmountable roadblocks, always accept the challenge head-on.

You will never be given more than you can handle, and although at the time it may seem overwhelming and perhaps even unbearable, when you accept whatever lies ahead without reservation you will overcome and even benefit from it. The long-term benefits will far outweigh the obstacles.

Accept and move toward your challenges and view them as a motivating factor in your journey to your predetermined goals.

Know that the lessons learned will be in direct proportion to the results realized.

FEBRUARY 18

There is a purpose and a reason for every person that comes into your life or that you encounter for one reason or another.

Whether you perceive the experience as positive or otherwise, there will be a benefit to you. The lesson may not yet be evident to you. You may not be ready for it or the time might not be right. On the flip side, you may, for several reasons, become immediately aware of the benefit or lesson.

Always leverage this newfound knowledge or rediscovered awareness.

FEBRUARY 19

———————————

The tremendously successful people on this planet are the ones that, when they get kicked, get up one last time.

Always stand tall; always project the success you deserve.

FEBRUARY 20

Take, or better yet make, time every week to invest in productive projects or initiatives—projects that will move you forward, upward, and closer to your ultimate goal.

You will need to develop worthwhile, quantified, duplicable, and easily monetizable initiatives.

FEBRUARY 21

Spend time every week with those that are important to you—your spouse, children, friends, and any person or people that are important to you and your forward growth and upward motion.

If those who are important to you are not close by, make a point of visiting them at least once a year. And go out and make, build, and nurture new productive and powerful relationships.

Refuse the temptation to put off spending time with those who you care for and who are important to your growth.

FEBRUARY 22

The primary component of nearly everything in our lives is communication. Effective communication, that is.

Be aware that there are numerous components to effective communication. Here is one that some of us seem to have an interesting time with—listening. Communication is a two-way street. You need to be able to listen and absorb what is being conveyed to you and then respond. We were given two ears and one mouth for a reason. Don't just hear—engage and listen. Avoid thinking about or formulating a response or rebuttal while the other person is still talking. If you do, you aren't really engaged in the conversation.

Be mindful that not everybody you come into contact with will hear, absorb, assimilate, or understand what you say, or are attempting to convey, in the way you intended it to be heard or understood.

Focus on always being a top-notch, effective communicator, ensuring that those you are communicating with grasp and understand your message as you intended it.

FEBRUARY 23

As you overcome small fears and meet with equal-sized successes, you will gain the courage to tackle the big fears that are holding you back. The bigger the fears you challenge and overcome, the larger and more profound your successes will become. They are in equal proportion.

FEBRUARY 24

About you.

No matter who you are, where you come from, where you live, who your parents are, how much education you have or don't have, how much money you have or don't have, or what someone may or may not have told you...

YOU ARE INCREDIBLE AND YOU DESERVE THE VERY BEST THAT LIFE HAS TO OFFER!

FEBRUARY 25

The only real control that we have is control over ourselves. You really are your own boss. In a vast majority of cases, you have the ability to determine the outcomes of most of the situations you find yourself in or become involved with.

Once you understand and master this gifted skill, and only then, can you really make the difference that you were meant to make. Relax and be confident in your ability to positively impact any situation in which you may find yourself.

Refuse to allow anyone or anything to impact you in any way, other than initiating your emotionally controlled response.

Be a positive force, have a calming impact, and leave a lasting positive impression.

FEBRUARY 26

While most have given up on their goals – tenacity having been deleted from their vocabulary – you are different. You remain focused and driven. You are tenacious, and you persist notwithstanding what you may encounter or what challenges you may face on your journey toward the achievement of your Big Hairy Audacious Goal.

FEBRUARY 27

The quality of your life is dependent on how engaged you are in living. Be constantly "on" in all you do.

Sleepwalking through life, or permitting someone or something else to dominate what you do or don't do, will lead you into a life of misery.

Live YOUR life and manifest YOUR dreams with a focus on service to others.

FEBRUARY 28

Live life big.

Be authentic!

Give it all you've got, then give it twice that.

Be real.

Aim big and take big risks.

Live life as if there is no tomorrow.

FEBRUARY 29

(Just in Case) or Your Bonus

Treat every connection as a gift, as that is exactly what it is. Every single person you are blessed to interact with, no matter how brief that meeting may be, presents an opportunity to share your gifts.

Always leave others with a positive experience, no matter their disposition or response. Always leave positivity and encouragement behind and, in some situations, perhaps only a genuine and heartfelt smile.

Always seek a connection, and you will make connections. When you make a deep connection with an individual, which doesn't happen often, hold onto it and don't let go. Deep connections are the spice of life and the stimulus that we need to make a difference.

March

Focus

"Focus is at the foundation of happiness and achievement. Focus on your goal to the exclusion of all outside distractions."
– Shawn Shewchuk

For the month of March, we are focusing on focus. Our lives are rife with distractions, every one of them designed to take our focus away from what is important. Only you can decide what is important, based on what you have resolved you want your life to look like and what you want your outcomes to be. Nothing is as important as your goals and the steps you take to get there.

MARCH 1

Inevitably, you will be faced with a terrier barrier, or what you may perceive as an insurmountable challenge. Double down and do whatever it takes to kick through it.

You will find that when you start moving, when you take the first step, when you face it and deal with it, it will likely not be as large as it initially appeared.

MARCH 2

When you develop deep and meaningful relationships with a select number of like-minded people that you connect with deeply, you become accomplices in each other's success.

Focus on always meeting new people—people that are driven and motivated to achieve more than what society considers average or good. Surround yourself with great people, rely on these people, and invite them to rely on you, and you will witness results beyond anything that you could have possibly imagined or dreamed.

MARCH 3

The largest gap in our lives is between what we know and what we do.

Most adults and even children have a fairly good idea of what they should be doing, but most don't do it.

Resolve to act on your knowledge and awareness. Fill the gap with those predetermined action steps.

MARCH 4

_____

Failure is your tuition. The God or the universe chooses to teach necessary lessons at the right time, although we may not always agree.

Don't seek failure, but when faced with it run toward it, challenge it, learn from it, and overcome it.

MARCH 5

What you see is what you get. You have likely heard that statement before, and it's true. What you focus on, you get more of.

There is some newer information that indicates that what you observe, your mind automatically works toward, making the same thing a reality for you. Be mindful of what you are watching and observing, as it will impact your outcomes.

MARCH 6

We've been taught that practice makes perfect, and it's true. I often tell people that the first rule of success is repetition.

This can be a double-edged sword or work for both good and bad. Always be aware of what you are practicing and repeating. Your objective in this is to become great at the right things. Avoid the repeated performance of what you know you don't want. Otherwise, you will become increasingly good at that.

Repeat and constantly practice so that the good becomes great.

MARCH 7

Dig deep today and every day. This gives you the power to create and develop what's truly important in your life.

Don't focus on recognition or prestige. When you give all you can and then more, the recognition and other benefits will follow.

Here are the important areas:
-Building your legacy
-Making a big difference
-Engaging in something meaningful
-Having a lasting impact
-Having significance
-Creating something special

In the end, these will matter far more and hold much greater significance than the material aspects of life that so many put such a great deal of focus and energy on.

MARCH 8

When you are ready for actively seeking and anticipating great opportunities, they will show up. You will need to become engaged and involved.

To clarify, most people aren't ready for any type of opportunity, and, of course, if you aren't prepared and seeking out opportunities, you won't see them.

No matter the situation, real or perceived, seek out the opportunities. They are always there; you'll need to be prepared to take them on.

MARCH 9

_____

Daily target:

Every day, make a point to take steps to be better than you were the day before; to understand better and to serve more and, as a result, to accomplish more.

Just imagine what you will accomplish when you implement this as part of your daily routine.

MARCH 10

Great advice is extremely valuable and really is a big part of your ongoing education. Always be seeking great advice.

Education and awareness are to you what fertilizer is to plants. It organically causes growth.

Advice from your coach, mentor, or other known and trusted sources must be accepted, applied, and implemented.

MARCH 11

The generally accepted notion that it takes years to accomplish certain ideals in life is not reality. It is societal conditioning.

It's been proven time after time—you can accomplish more in one day than you can likely even fathom at this moment.

Your perspective, focus, direction, pace, understanding, and self-expectation may need to be augmented, but it's entirely possible. You can do in a day what the average person will likely struggle to do in a workweek.

Now that you know this, focus only on the next sentence. Pick the big task and resolve to complete it in a day. Go and do it!

I believe in you!

MARCH 12

When you are seeking solutions – an opportunity, wealth, happiness, or any other goal that you may have, whether of a material nature or not – you need to be aware of the following guideline.

Expend energy only on worthwhile and productive causes. Your direction and speed of travel are determined in part by the energy exerted. Be constantly aware of the amount of energy that you expend and ensure that the energy spent on your journey is constructive and beneficial.

MARCH 13

Devote yourself to being the best at everything you touch and every initiative you become engaged in.

Taking that first step is important, and it leads to great things. You have to start!

Of equal or perhaps even greater importance is that you complete what you've started prior to moving on. Of course, how you finish speaks to your level of dedication and engagement.

MARCH 14

The opinion that you hold of yourself may be dramatically different than the perception that others may have of you.

Develop, collaborate on, perfect, and proactively promote and protect your personal brand. This is how those who don't know you begin to get to know you. This is your reputation.

Before he left this planet, my Dad taught me something that will stay with me forever. He said, "Shawn, the only thing you take with you is your name."

MARCH 15

We talk about thinking, and, as you know, most people don't think. Or at the most, they think just enough to get by. So, it would stand to reason that if you are going to think, you need to do it in a big way.

It takes no more energy to think big than it does to think small.

MARCH 16

Confident people focus on opportunities, and for those who are confident, change represents opportunity.

MARCH 17

Life is a performance; you are therefore a performer.

As a performer, your focus is different from that of those who aren't performers. Non-performers focus on the obstacles while performers focus on results.

MARCH 18

Every problem or perceived challenge is masking as a fantastic opportunity.

Always focus on and seek out the opportunities.

MARCH 19

There are times when just being quiet and still is a rewarding experience. We often get caught up in the noise and rush of our lives—much of which, in the larger scheme of life, really doesn't matter.

Take the time to listen, to engage beyond the day-to-day needs of our lives, and to tap into ideas and resources that are available to all of us.

Massive rewards are in store for you.

MARCH 20

Why do some people make it, and why do some fall short? These are big questions, and I'm going to give you the answers. Take the time to study these in depth. I talk a great deal about these in my first book, *Change Your Mind, Change Your Results.*

Number 1: You have to know and be clear on your WHY.
Number 2: You need to know where you are going; you need a clearly defined destination.
Number 3: You need to develop predetermined and bite-sized action steps.
Number 4: You have to execute those predetermined action steps.
Number 5: You should celebrate your successes.

MARCH 21

_____

Expect the best!

Our focus has a great deal to do with our position or where we are in our lives, businesses/careers, and, of course, our relationships.

Our expectation of the outcome in any area of our lives has a direct impact on the results that we experience.

What do you expect?

MARCH 22

Throughout your life, you may encounter someone who disagrees with you on one point or another, and that is alright. Wouldn't it be a boring existence if we were all of the same opinions?

To disagree with an opinion or position isn't a conflict and doesn't have to become one. Always be the bigger person and refuse to permit the situation to escalate, for that will benefit no one.

Become an expert at knowing when a disagreement is looming and redirect it so that it doesn't grow into something more. A difference of opinions or viewpoints only becomes more when it is permitted to. The onus is on you, not the other party, to head things in the right direction. Remember, you know how to deal with disagreements, and others may not yet be aware.

Take the high road and be the leader through your example for those with whom you come into contact.

MARCH 23

My grandmother was, by societal norms, not educated, and in broken English about a week before she left this planet, she gave me the following advice.

"Love God. Do what you want to do in life (career/business), get good friends, work extremely hard, and you will make it."

In other words, acknowledge your creator, find something that you are passionate about, associate with those that support and motivate you (not detractors), work harder than anyone else, and you will be successful. You will get to where you want to be when it's your time.

This is great advice for all of us to adhere to and follow.

MARCH 24

Every time you open your eyes in the morning, it is a gift. Be thankful and show your gratitude through how you think, communicate, and act.

Through an attitude of gratitude, you convey to those around you that you're living a life of awesomeness. Remember that gratitude is one of two of the most powerful forces available to us.

Being grateful is the only way to thrive.

MARCH 25

Dedication, tenacity, focus, and hard work are the engines that power you and move you forward to the long-term rewards of achievement and success.

Integrity, honesty, and ethics are the fuel that powers your engines.

In order to get there, you need a defined destination.

MARCH 26

We all have some form and level of stress. How do you deal with it?

Stress is the level of energy exerted to resist our current situation. Stop resisting and learn how to move in the flow.

MARCH 27

Understanding finances will change your outlook and fortune. The following will eliminate the stress surrounding money, finances, and income.

Escape the time-for-money trap. Ensure that you get paid for your value and not your time.

MARCH 28

Improvise, don't perfect.

The above statement is loaded.

1. First, find the path to deal with a perceived challenge. There is always a solution!

2. Always seek opportunities in whatever situation you may be facing. There are always opportunities.

3. Start now! Don't wait until you or the situation or something else is perfect. Perfection doesn't exist.

Always find a way. Be accountable to yourself, those around you, and your coach.

MARCH 29

When you become wholly accountable for every aspect of your life, career/business, and relationships, things change for the better.

This shift is always on the positive side of your life. The reason: accountability is the opposite of procrastination.

Strategic Accountability™ breeds action.

MARCH 30

This is BIG!

To improve your results, you need to change your attitude.

Your attitude is comprised of the following three things: your thoughts, feelings, and actions.

If you've ever heard someone say that they just met someone with a bad attitude, it simply means that one of the three components noted above is out of alignment.

Be aware of these three factors in your own life.

MARCH 31

Most people stop before they even start.

Here are three great nuggets of sound advice that I received from one of my mentors many years ago.

- Avoid or ignore anything and everything that may be a hindrance or that may take you off course. Don't internalize the input of detractors—they don't have your best interests in mind.

- Refuse to allow ANYONE or ANYTHING to stop you from starting.

- Action trumps perfection! Don't wait for it to be perfect or for the timing to be exactly right. There may never be a perfect time, and waiting for perfection is a form of procrastination.

April

Service

"It is through service that we raise one another higher and higher."
– Shawn Shewchuk

For the month of April, our word is service. For those in need – your family, your team, and, of course, those you have the privilege of working with (clients, customers, students, etc.) – your service should always be at the forefront. Place an emphasis on being of service no matter where you are, who you are with, or your initial reaction.

APRIL 1

Only fools refuse to listen, absorb, and act. Only fools know everything and propagate misinformation to anyone that will pay attention. Narcissism, pompousness, and disengagement are traits of a fool.

Always listen. If the information is congruent with and aligned to your values, absorb it. It takes a confident and wise person to know that they will never know everything. An intelligent and aware individual speaks only of what he or she is 100% certain and can back up. A gifted individual is always focused on others and how he or she can be of service—always.

APRIL 2

You have been given the privilege of serving for another day. Honor that gift by going above and beyond and giving more than you ever have before. Give more than you believe you should, give more than you want to, and give more than you were paid for.

APRIL 3

Always give, even when you don't need to, don't want to, or aren't required to.

Always give more – more that you were paid for – even if you don't want to or feel you don't have time to.

Always deliver more. Always ensure you deliver a wow.

Always go the extra mile—there aren't many others along the extra mile.

Your rewards will be more than you can possibly even fathom.

APRIL 4

Every day is a great day to make someone else's day better.

Resolve to in some way make today better for at least two people. It's even more interesting when that's a stranger, as it's completely unexpected.

Perhaps it's as simple as a smile or holding the door open for someone. Of course, it might be a much greater or more impactful gesture, which is admirable.

No matter the size, the effect is always the same—gratitude. Even if it's not articulated back to you, know you've made a positive difference in someone's life.

APRIL 5

Life is about learning. Always be ready for, open to, and accepting of new information. Be ready to accept life lessons from everyone you encounter even if at times you don't expect it. Be always cognizant of every situation; life's finer details will reveal themselves to you and teach you immeasurable lessons.

Some of the most important life lessons come from those we least expect—children. Children have this unique innocence that speaks to us on a higher level. If you're aware, you'll benefit immensely.

APRIL 6

Once you've established your big-picture goal or destination your energy, focus, and direction will shift. What you are required to do to achieve your goal becomes more important than what you thought was important prior to the clarification of your goal.

This perceptible change is a part of becoming the person it was always intended you become. Go with it, no matter where it leads you.

APRIL 7

Problems are really life-changing opportunities waiting to be exposed.

It's how you choose to view the problems and engage in leveraging the opportunity that will make the difference.

It's up to you.

APRIL 8

You will make this journey but once. How you make your way along the road of life is up to you.

You can tiptoe through on the hope that you will arrive at death's door without being badly bruised, or you can live a life that is full and complete, achieving all of your goals and fulfilling your untamed dreams.

APRIL 9

Teamwork, whether in life, business, or career, is imperative for sustained growth. Without the right team in place – without the support network around you – you or your business will encounter unnecessary and perhaps even insurmountable challenges.

Divide and conquer. Download and delegate a portion of the work to your team members, and it will become easier and quicker to accomplish.

Individuals without support will fall. Build a group of true and like-minded friends that believe in you and support you in whatever you choose to pursue, regardless of how crazy it may seem.

APRIL 10

Celebrate the milestones of life.

Celebrate achievement.

Be grateful for the gift of time; be always aware of its fragility and fleetingness.

Leverage the strength of your successes to catapult you forward to your next big achievement.

Make every day a celebration!

APRIL 11

If you are basing your goals only on money, you may find yourself lost.

Wealth is more than money; it encompasses everything in life.
- ✓ Health
- ✓ Family
- ✓ Friends
- ✓ Relationships
- ✓ Material things
- ✓ Your business or career
- ✓ Money
- ✓ The ability to give back or pay it forward.

Money is neither bad nor good, it just is. It exists simply as a tool. It or anything else should never become an obsession or your sole reason for existence.

It's not about the money—it's about what money can do for you and those you care for and love. Money also exists for us to make a difference in the lives of those that can't speak for or help themselves.

APRIL 12

The meaning of life, to some, is an enigma. The reality is that the meaning of life is simple. It's about what we give, not what we get or take.

Place a focus on giving!

APRIL 13

There are 168 hours in every week. Imagine what our world would be like if every person on this planet utilized just one of those hours to help those that needed a hand up.

- ✓ Family
- ✓ Friends
- ✓ Animals
- ✓ The hungry
- ✓ The homeless

The list is truly endless. I suggest you make a promise to yourself to commit to giving as much as you can to make a difference for just one creature.

APRIL 14

Your levels of growth and corresponding results are determined by the level of service that you provide.

Increase your level of service to increase your results.

If you focus on how much you can acquire, your experience may not be what you desire.

Real and lasting success is the result of what we give, not how much we can take.

APRIL 15

"What are you doing today?" An innocent but important question from my two-year-old son; a question that we should be asking ourselves every morning.

And perhaps we should be asking ourselves what we are doing on a more regular basis, as in every minute of every day. Is what you are doing productive, and is what you are doing moving you in the direction of your goals?

APRIL 16

To achieve more and to get more, and to obtain what few others have, you will have to do what few others are willing to do. You will need to commit, become engaged, sacrifice, and become 100% accountable.

You will need a work ethic unlike anything you have ever had before. The great thing is, you can make anything happen. You just have to commit and take the first step!

APRIL 17

Take a stand!

Stand for something worthwhile, something that you and those you love will be proud of and something that leaves a trail long after you are gone—your legacy of service!

Take a stand to do the right thing, without exception.

APRIL 18

The following is always true, whether you believe it to be so or not.

To try is to fail. That is a fact.

Always commit to and be proud of what you accomplish. Do or do not… Period!

APRIL 19

You will fail and likely continue to encounter failure. The key is to gain an understanding that failure is a significant component of success. Without failure, you would never succeed, nor would you gain anything in the process.

Run toward failure when you are faced with it; learn from it and implement the necessary shifts as a result of the lessons learned.

Success is so much sweeter because of failure.

View failure as your tuition.

APRIL 20

You need tools to make "it" happen. One of those tools, an especially important tool in your arsenal, is the mastermind.

You need people. We've all heard that two heads are better than one. Very simply, this is one principle that you would be wise to follow.

Mastermind, brainstorm, find solutions, network, solve problems, encourage, and motivate each other.

APRIL 21

Follow up on yesterday's entry.

Vast amounts of knowledge, inspiration, motivation, and guidance are gained when the mastermind principle is utilized.

Engage and mastermind with like-minded and motivated people on a regular basis. The results will be astoundingly impressive.

APRIL 22

Set aside time for you to share, help, and give back in some way to someone who needs it. This could mean a suggestion (if sought out), physical help, or a smile and perhaps even something anonymous. Always donate generously of your time and resources.

APRIL 23

Let your passion become stronger than your fears.

It will change your outcomes.

APRIL 24

Look up, not down. Look ahead, not behind you.

Seek and find more fulfilling opportunities.

Determine additional areas of service.

APRIL 25

Don't let detractors prevent you from going down the road less traveled.

You choose your path. You determine your outcomes.

APRIL 26

You have infinite reservoirs of potential.

Ask your coach to help you in excavating and utilizing your immense and amazing gifts.

APRIL 27

Share your time, your knowledge, your gifts, and your opportunities.

Your returns will be in direct proportion to the level of service you provide and the positive impact that you deliver.

APRIL 28

View and treat each day as a new opportunity and a fresh start.

Create lasting memories and positive impacts every day.

APRIL 29

Holding in will not serve you. Anything that you attempt to hold in or suppress will have the opposite effect of what you intended the outcome to be.

The stark truth is that we rarely if ever hold in anything good and powerful. We suppress only those emotions that are negative in nature.

The unintentional but inevitable manifestation of suppressed emotions can be detrimental to you and those around you that you love. Suppression is always the result of an event, real or previewed, from the past.

Holding anything in is poisonous and deadly.

You cannot change the past.

Release that which you cannot change.

Embrace change. Change is opportunity.

APRIL 30

Let go of anything that doesn't serve you. Just because it once worked or you feel attached to it doesn't justify holding onto something that will obstruct your view of and progress toward your objective.

Refuse to allow anything to stand in your way.

May

Freedom

"Every human seeks freedom. Freedom is defined in the following three ways.
The ability to do what you want, when you want, and with whom you want."
– Shawn Shewchuk

For the month of May, we are placing a focus on the F-Word, which is always on our minds but rarely discussed. It was always intended that we live a life that is free. Freedom – your version of freedom – is the motivating factor in getting you started and achieving your goals.

MAY 1

You will undoubtedly face challenges from time to time. These may be real or perceived. Either way, what's important is how you deal with them.

When the going gets tough, no matter how you feel or what most might do, there is only one thing for you to do—keep going no matter what.

You will get through it. On the other side is freedom.

MAY 2

While money and material possessions are necessary and important, time with those you love and care about must be at the top of the priority list.

There is no one who on their deathbed says, "I should have spent more time working" or regrets not acquiring more "things."

MAY 3

You are powerful!

You are capable!

You have everything it takes to become who you want to be.

Develop faith in yourself and your abilities. Practice growing that faith by stretching your boundaries and challenging yourself to attain larger objectives.

If initially it feels impossible, that's a strong indication that you are headed in the right direction.

MAY 4
_____

Make friends everywhere you go.

It's people that make life interesting and worthwhile.

It all starts with a smile.

MAY 5

Great people are an indication of a great life. Put yourself in a position to meet and engage with great people.

Surround yourself with phenomenal people. Grow with like-minded people. Always be of service to everyone you interact with.

MAY 6

Put effort and time into building strong, powerful, and highly trusting relationships.

Your growth, your business/career, and your financial fitness are dependent upon the relationships that you build and nurture.

Your relational capital is one of the most important assets that you have.

MAY 7

Every experience throughout our lives is an opportunity to learn.

The test is what we do with the takeaway lessons gleaned from our unique life journey.

MAY 8

We are all faced with pressures from time to time. These are situations and interesting opportunities that mold our future.

Being open to these learning experiences is important, and how we function when faced with these life-changing scenarios determines the person we become.

When faced with these opportunities, the only path that you can choose is to do whatever it takes. You need to perform as if your life depends on that—because it does.

MAY 9

Spend, treasure, and make the most of the time you have with those who are important to you.

When you really take a moment to assess your life, you find that the moments that make everything worthwhile are those spent with family members and friends that you love and care for.

MAY 10

Living the same day, the same month, or the same year on repeat won't change the outcomes.

So many live the same year 80 times and call it a life.

Change it up, embrace the new, and live life on your terms.

MAY 11

Refuse to permit pebbles to become boulders. What initially appears as real may only be mirages and figments of your imagination.

Your execution and accomplishment of predetermined objectives must be a priority. The size of your goal is always a motivation rather than an impediment to achievement.

MAY 12

It's Mother's Day.

Give thanks. Without her, you wouldn't be here. It's that simple.

MAY 13

───────────────

Your gifts are unique to you and are unlike anyone else's gifts.

Our mission in life should always be to serve, through our gifts, the amazing humans that we share this planet with.

MAY 14

Most of us search for something; this something is what Scott Fay calls our "Sweet Spot."

When you find your calling, or in some cases create your calling, it's important to do one thing. Let your true calling be your guide.

MAY 15

Make time every day to learn, grow, and feed your mind.

Your physical health, longevity, financial fitness, mental acuity, and spiritual acumen are 100% dependent upon the continued expansion of your awareness.

MAY 16

Your subconscious mind is your power center. You have only just scratched the surface of your immense potential.

Become engaged by excavating and then tapping into your deep reservoir of potential. You will shock yourself!

If desiring to progress at a higher level is your focus, a good coach can and will be an invaluable asset.

It's GO time!

MAY 17

_____

The main thing is to keep the main thing the main thing.

MAY 18
_____

The world needs more open-minded people.

The world needs people that think.

The world needs more independent thinkers.

The world needs visionaries.

The world needs you to step up and be the you that you were intended to be.

MAY 19

There is at least one reason you are here, and there is at least one reason you're still here.

You have infinite potential. Excavate, utilize, and leverage that potential. The single most important reason you are here is to serve.

Living a life of service to others is the cornerstone of becoming the person it was always intended you grow into.

MAY 20

———————

Unlock genius; tap into and listen to your intuition. Then do what it says! 😊

MAY 21

Good enough isn't good enough.

You have been gifted with the ability, potential, and talent to perform at any level. Go way up the ladder and go beyond good.

This is true no matter who you are.

MAY 22

One of us is not more special than another.

We were all created equal. Some of us, however, have decided up the ante; to accomplish more in less time and to leave a lasting and positive impact.

What have you decided?

MAY 23

Today and every day, unleash your genius onto the world.

You are here to serve; you accomplish this through selflessly giving of your gifts.

MAY 24

What we say and what we think are often different—just saying something doesn't make it so.

That is why we need to communicate clearly and concisely.

Clear communication is key to achieving our goals and objectives.

If there are things that are unclear to you, have the courage to seek clarification.

MAY 25

Every person, no matter the time spent on this planet, has a calling.

A large part of that calling is to serve those that we are fortunate enough to share this planet with.

MAY 26

Challenges come in all sizes for all of us.

The higher we reach, the more we are challenged, and this is good. Grow through challenges.

Everything molds us to be the person we become.

Remember, life tests those who dream big.

MAY 27

_____

The discussion, the research, and the planning are as complete they can be.

So, leave everything but the action steps behind.

Today is the day that you start doing!

MAY 28

When we manage our internal conversations and become aware of our environment, we increase our external influence.

Your influence is contagious!

MAY 29

You've heard it before. The question is: Did you listen?

Known as your intuition, the small voice, Holy Spirit, and so much more—this is your internal guidance system.

Your guidance system can only work with what it has. Educate, train, and arm yourself with every tool that you can. The higher your awareness, the more accurate your intuition will become.

MAY 30

_____

Take a moment to say thank you.

Live in gratitude always.

MAY 31

Be true to those you care for and love; to those that you interact with daily through your business or career.

It all starts with being true to yourself!

June

Consistency

"To build a world-class anything, the one constant must be consistency,
even in the face of adversity or unprecedented success."
– **Shawn Shewchuk**

For the month of June, we examine consistency. Those that went before us have left a path to achieve something world class. This is accomplished through small changes with a focus on daily activities that create the paradigm shift that world class demands.

JUNE 1

Your value exceeds anything you can possibly imagine.

You are valuable beyond comparison and more important than anything else on the planet.

Pass it on.

JUNE 2

Be relaxed, calm, and aware. When you show up this way, life becomes more of what it was intended to be. Ideas, solutions, and the direction of travel will become evident.

You have everything you need to complete any task, solve any problem, and achieve any goal. You just need to allow this to come to the surface.

JUNE 3

What you allow in is related to your output and results. For every success and every result, there is a level of input and sacrifice required.

You will need to decide how much you are willing to put in and sacrifice for what you genuinely want in life, business or career, and relationships.

JUNE 4

It's not how much comes in, it's about what you do with what comes in.

The more you get, the more you'll want and desire. While that is a good thing, it should be tempered with an awareness of what your priorities are.

JUNE 5

Of utmost importance is to always pay yourself first. No matter what you do, no matter what you have accomplished in life, no matter what anyone may tell you, keep this at the forefront in your rituals and habits.

Make it natural to set aside at least 10% of everything you bring in. Never touch this amount, no matter how tempted you may be.

Most of all, never fear or worry that you will be unable to continue to function without the 10%. You will find that you neither need it nor miss it.

JUNE 6

It's not about the volume, it's about the connection.

Strive to establish and nurture deep connections.

JUNE 7

Every day is a celebration of your uniqueness, abilities, and accomplishments.

Celebrate every day!

JUNE 8

Never stop learning, growing, building, and increasing your awareness. Awareness, after all, is knowledge.

JUNE 9
_____

Build people, not businesses or bank accounts.

JUNE 10

You don't hire great people. Great people and teams are always encouraged, nurtured, coached, and celebrated.

Building a great team is always a test of a true leader. Some will come and go—how you lead determines your long-term contribution and outcomes.

JUNE 11

What you see may not actually be what is. Before responding, acting, and or even correcting, be certain that what you see is real and not a mirage.

JUNE 12

Awareness is knowledge. The more extensive your knowledge, the more precise and on target your decisions will be.

Everything in your life is predicated on the decisions you make.

JUNE 13

Accountability is key.

Resolve right now to give yourself the space to develop the focus that is required to see through all the hype and to focus on what are truly important possibilities and opportunities.

Take control of your situation today!

JUNE 14

When it seems like there's so much coming at you (even when it's positive), and you're experiencing overload, stay focused on the big picture of your objective.

You will come through triumphant and successful. You'll have learned an immense amount and are better prepared for the next big adventure.

JUNE 15

There are times when you'll be left with little choice but to ramp up your activity level.

At the time, it may seem counterintuitive, perhaps even counterproductive, but know that there is a reason for the increase in your activities. It will become apparent at some future date.

Take it in stride; accept and be grateful for the opportunities.

Be aware that a refined focus may be your best friend, especially when you believe that you've hit the full mark.

You have at least triple the capacity that you think or believe you do.

JUNE 16

It's Father's Day.

The development of balance and synergy requires that you be engaged, awake, and ready for the opportunities as they present themselves. In addition, you must leverage the time you are allotted.

Devote your time to only the activities that are of the highest priority. Engage in activities that are important to you—that are productive and what you want to be doing.

If you aren't quite sure where you want to be yet, that's alright. Just become the absolute best at what you are doing, right where you are.

JUNE 17

Productivity is defined as any activity or action step that moves you in the direction of your goal or objective.

If you are engaged in any non-productive activities, download, delegate, or automate them. Divest yourself of them immediately.

JUNE 18

Simplicity. For you to be highly effective and create sustainable results, you need to really take to heart the title of my first book, *CHANGE YOUR MIND, CHANGE YOUR RESULTS*.

When you utterly understand this, it really will make the difference between where you are and where you want and deserve to be.

JUNE 19

Throughout history, there has been universal acceptance and agreement of this one principle.

We become what we think about!

In our unnecessarily over-complicated lives, most people seem to have a difficult time grasping this seemingly simple but proven tenet of the successful.

JUNE 20

Believe me when I tell you—you need help. We all do!

Accountability is the key.

You need to be accountable to yourself first, and then you should be held accountable to and by your coach.

Bottom line: you need a coach. The most successful people today have a coach; sometimes more than one.

The right coach makes THE difference.

Don't go for the cheap options—you'll end up with less than stellar results plus you'll lose your investment. Make the best investment that you can make; invest in you. Work with the BEST there is. Pay your coach handsomely, as you obviously want to work with the absolute best.

JUNE 21

───────────────

EVERY DAY, before your feet touch the floor in the morning, say THANK YOU! Begin now to always say THANK YOU!

No matter how much or how little you think you have, there is always something for you to give thanks for. How about this: you woke up this morning.

If you draw breath, make gratitude your attitude. You'll be grateful you did!

JUNE 22

It's true! Small changes produce big results.

Start with small changes. Know that real change and the results of change have a gestation period.

It takes time, effort, energy, faith, tenacity, determination, and at times even more.

JUNE 23

You have the ability to accept, reject, or ignore anything (thoughts or ideas) that come at you.

Consciously choose to avoid negative influences of any kind. Surround yourself with the type of information and people that promote your ongoing growth.

JUNE 24

Study tremendously successful and wealthy people. You will find that all are service-centric, with purpose and focus.

You will also note one important fact: they associate and spend time with people that are driven, motivated, and successful. You become who you associate with. Keep this in mind as you establish, develop, and grow your relationships and friendships.

JUNE 25

Pay attention!

Ensure that you have a clear understanding of your destination. Base your actions on this awareness and knowledge.

Always be learning and able to assess any situation quickly; decide based on the information gained as a result of the assessment.

Being quick on your feet means that you can answer questions and make important decisions without dissecting the information into indiscernible pieces.

JUNE 26

Great investments produce a big ROI (return on investment). The best investment that you can ever make is an ongoing investment in yourself.

Your investment will include the following components to start: Time - Energy - Spirituality - Finances. You will, in turn, see as large a return as you are prepared to invest.

Always have a coach, always be involved in a directed mastermind, always spend time sharing, and always spend time on you. Always be ready to invest in you! You are worth it.

Always focus on the outcomes that you want, desire, and deserve. When you take the quantified action steps that lead you in the direction of your goal, the relatively minor investments that you make will pale by comparison to the outcomes you will realize.

Start investing in you today! Don't turn sideways and don't ask questions—just take the step to achieve your goals!

JUNE 27

So many of us remain permanently stuck. This is unnecessary and can be easily remedied. You can cure yourself of the condition known as paralysis by analysis.

When you are faced with a decision, you must very quickly weigh the pros and cons and make the decision. Quickly making an informed decision will lead to many opportunities that you would otherwise miss.

Paralysis by analysis is a dream killer.

JUNE 28

Risk promotes growth. No matter what you may have been told, you cannot avoid risk. If you attempt to avoid risk, you will stop growing.

You can and should manage risk. This very simply means that you weigh both sides of the decision and, notwithstanding the risk involved, make the decision that makes the most sense. There will always be risk—just manage it to minimize it.

Manage risk but don't attempt to avoid risk. Risk represents growth.

JUNE 29

If your vision is opaque and vague, your results will be lackluster and mediocre.

The clearer the picture you hold, the more vibrant that image is and the less anxiety, fear, and doubt you will experience. A clear picture of your destination or goal will give you the added confidence that you need to advance in the right direction.

JUNE 30

No matter what happens, no matter how you're being tested, no matter how hard it gets, and no matter what anyone else may say... NEVER, ever give up!

July

People

"Whether serving, adding value, and contributing... it's always all about people."
– Shawn Shewchuk

For the month of June, we examine people—you, me, and every other human on this planet. We were placed here for one reason, and that is very simply to serve others. Be aware that this is a two-way street. You need to understand your value and the value of what you deliver before you deliver it. Otherwise, you do others and yourself a disservice.

JULY 1

It's Canada Day. Happy Birthday, Canada.

Just as imperative as water is for you and your longevity... so too is your time spent in solitude, learning, and educating yourself.

Spending just one hour out of 24 can make the difference in your results.

JULY 2

_____

Game Changers make and dedicate their time to what, for them, are priorities. These priorities are detailed and quantified.

Game Changers make every attempt to predetermine what is vital and time-sensitive, and then develop and execute that plan.

JULY 3

Game Changers know that it takes more than the individual. Game Changers develop, nurture, and continuously grow and leverage strong, powerful high-trust relationships.

It's been said that your network equals your net worth.

It's all about people, not about money or the state of the business.

People are business, and business is people.

JULY 4

It's Independence Day in the USA. Happy Independence Day!

Truly dedicated entrepreneurs, a.k.a. Game Changers, are aware of risks and what it takes to prevail. They are prepared for risks and will do whatever it takes to succeed, without violating the rights of others.

JULY 5

Things are never quite as bad as they may initially appear. The situations that cause us challenges or sorrow are exactly what gives us the ability to develop the strength and tenacity to persevere in the face of any circumstance.

JULY 6

Spend time on you. Invest in you. Engage in activities that are invigorating and revitalizing and allow you to become re-energized.

When you have what you need, you will be able to accomplish more and do it in less time.

JULY 7

Always focus on giving and how you can be of service. Find ways to contribute and add value to another human.

Showing up in this way will reflect on your relationships, business, or career. This is the sole reason that you are on this planet. The reality is, it's the only reason we're all here on this little planet that we call home.

JULY 8

When you feel that you need strength, bear in mind how we attain strength. We become stronger through the act of giving, of serving, and of being a source of strength for those around us—for everyone that we encounter on a daily basis.

Immense strength is attained through becoming that unshakable source for others.

JULY 9

You need to commit to conscious, minute-by-minute micro-decisions. This series of decisions will control what you do in every aspect of your life. In other words, you are re-taking control of your life and the decisions that govern your life. You then own your outcomes.

Unquestionably, the decisions you make determine your results. This applies to all areas of life. Remember, life is inclusive. By that I mean this will impact your health, relationships, business or career, and a myriad of other areas.

The decisions are yours!

JULY 10

Reject thoughts and ideas that limit what you believe is possible. Choose to focus only on what is possible.

Refuse to blindly accept the opinions of others.

JULY 11

———————

Growth is critical to fulfillment in business, career, relationships, and all areas of life.

Are you growing?

JULY 12

Open your mind to what you really want in life and allow yourself to dream. Un-cap your creativity, which all of us were gifted with, and allow yourself to soar.

Dreamers are builders.

JULY 13

You can create your own economy in any economic time and any situation.

You are unable to control what anyone else is going to do. Forget competition and become creative in your approaches.

There are always opportunities. You will just have to refine your approach.

JULY 14

Your thoughts create your life. Yesterday created today and today creates tomorrow.

Know that every decision that you make impacts you, your family, and ultimately your entire life.

JULY 15

Everything starts with awareness, and it expands as you consciously make choices rather than just floating through on the same old routine.

The status quo will not serve you in your pursuit of growth and achievement. We are growth-seeking organisms. Determine to always seek out and leverage new and growth-related opportunities no matter how daunting the appearance.

JULY 16

Throughout the process of building the life you desire and deserve, you would do well to bear in mind the following.

The attainment of any one goal is not the destination. As a matter of fact, it's not at all about the destination. It's entirely about the experience, lessons learned on the journey, relationships made and nurtured, and the progression of what is deemed a worthy ideal.

JULY 17

_____

Every encounter with a fellow human being should be laced with gratitude and altruistic openness.

JULY 18

Kindness trumps all else. No matter how difficult it may seem, give unconditionally from your unlimited reservoir of kindness.

JULY 19

What you validate grows in others and in yourself. Focus your intentions on validating only the best.

JULY 20

_____

Your best motivation comes from within. Re-engage with your inner drive, the one that caused you to become the incredible high achiever that you are.

JULY 21

Enjoy investing time by doing what is important to you—those things you love. This is paramount to a lifetime of fulfillment and happiness.

JULY 22

Your fear will dissipate when you engage with the source, higher power, or God.

Fear is only an internal emotion that exists nowhere but in your mind. It is a learned reaction that can be controlled and only used for safety and security.

JULY 23

———————————

Your strength is always available to you, just outside of the box.

The roadmap to success is printed on the outside of the box. If you don't kick through the box, you may never experience what was intended for you.

JULY 24

Embrace your decision to become great. Deliberately abandon mediocrity. Allow yourself to experience greatness.

Every time you chose greatness over mediocrity, it becomes easier and begins to create a paradigm shift.

When you decide to accept this, it becomes your lifestyle.

JULY 25

When you believe in you, those you encounter will believe in you.

Belief is one of the intrinsic components of achieving real and lasting success.

JULY 26

Significance trumps success.

Significance changes you; your perspective and approach.

What do you do daily that is in alignment with your values and brings you the feeling that you have made a difference and had a positive impact?

Place an emphasis and focus on significance, and success will follow.

JULY 27

How you start your day determines how you live your day and then delivers the outcome of your day.

How do you start your day?

JULY 28

To change your current results, you need to make changes to what you do every day, every hour, and at times every minute.

More of the same gives you more of the same.

The reason that less than 2% of people are considered high achievers is that these 2% are willing to do something dramatically different. They are aware of and accept that they are engaging in an activity that the other 98% won't take on.

Are you willing to go against the norms?

JULY 29

_____

Today is your day to take risks. You need to make that leap and experience the rewards that come from living big.

JULY 30

Most people are waiting for opportunities to jump out and bite them. Not you. Your path is different.

Today and every day you take the path that creates opportunities. This will be your focus above all else.

JULY 31

_____

You can and should be open and always seeking opportunities. Be prepared to receive and take the necessary action steps to bring those opportunities from concept to fruition.

August

Personal **Development**

"Improvement is always a choice. Those that excel are driven by an irrevocable decision to be the best at their chosen task."
– Shawn Shewchuk

For the month of August, we are talking about personal development and diving deeply into the subject. Personal development, as it is known, is not something that should be left to an hour or two a week on the weekends. Your daily "High Leverage Activities" (HLAs) must include intentionality of focus and specifically dedicated time to grow and then reap the rewards associated with improvement.

AUGUST 1

The most important conversations that you will ever have will be the conversations that you have with yourself. You know—the ones where you decide on whether to do something BIG.

Being aware of the power you possess at all times (what you can bring to power and which affects every aspect of your life) is critical to all that transpires and all that will become real to and for you. These decisions include everything.

What you do. What you are going to do. The impact you will have. Your brand and reputation. Where you live. What you drive. The type of relationships that you create and nurture. Your romantic interests. Your sources of income. Your intellectual property. The success of your business or career. Your bank account. Your legacy.

We tend to be cautious, as we feel that risk is a bad thing. We tend to deliberate because, somehow, we have deceived ourselves into thinking that things are magically going to change. We sometimes wait for validation from someone else. We even seek advice from someone who has never been where we are and likely never will be.

As you probably already know, hugely successful people make instant decisions and rarely, if ever, change their minds. This is amazing advice that I was gifted with back when I made the decision to change my trajectory and outcomes.

Today is the day. Have the conversation and make the decision. This is where you decide that your life must change and you are making it happen... Now!

AUGUST 2

Perspective shift:

Your belief system has to change so that your paradigm changes. When this happens, your thoughts become more than just a dream and your new paradigm starts to take over.

Money, you can make more of—it is simply just a decision. Believe it!

AUGUST 3

Everything in life is predicated on the decisions that you make.

How happy you are, today and always. The strength and longevity of your relationships—personal and business. How you deal with challenges or perceived challenges as they show up in your life. The success of your business or career. Your ability to respond, rather than react, to situations as they arise.

The quality of friends that you have. The amount of money that you earn and, more importantly, keep. Your ability to live the lifestyle that you want, desire, and deserve.

The list could go on forever. Make your own list and determine what you want the outcomes to be and how you want to see your life evolve. You have the power. Make every decision count. Your list:

AUGUST 4

I'm told that, until a few hundred years ago, the word "priority" was always singular and there was no plural version. And it stands to reason that we should have *a* priority. In the alternative, perhaps a limited number of priorities. Should you choose the latter, which most humans do, you will need to limit it to 3.

I've been asked by a few people over the years to look at their priority lists. When they show me their lists, most are incredibly long (in one case, over 16 pages).

Your priority list should comprise a maximum of three items! Commit to those 3 priorities only and focus on them until they are complete or you have mastered them. Focus to the exclusion of all outside distractions.

Three priorities:

1._____

_____

2._____

_____

3._____

_____

AUGUST 5

An ongoing and intentional focus on Personal Development is the only way to change your outcomes.

Letting your old paradigm run your life will not serve you in any positive way. If you live your life according to the conditioning from your childhood, you will not experience the life you want and deserve.

AUGUST 6

_____

Step into the uncomfortable.

If you're serious about growing, you can't avoid risk. You can and should manage risk.

Every day, do at least one thing that takes you out of your box. Challenge yourself to grow. Embrace real change. Take risks.

What are you going to do today?

AUGUST 7

The results you want, and the life you deserve, require you to invest. The purpose of an investment is generally to get a return.

You need to invest the following:

-Time
-Energy
-Effort
-Money

The investment with the greatest returns is the one with a major and ongoing investment in you.

AUGUST 8

Real change requires that you step off the hamster wheel.

Create a goal that forces you to grow. Remember that this is the sole purpose of a goal.

Reverse engineer that goal so you are crystal clear on what needs to happen yearly, monthly, daily, and hourly. Develop a detailed plan which, while not necessarily perfect, outlines what those accountability checkpoints are.

Then execute that plan consistently to experience the results that you deserve.

AUGUST 9

Constantly work on you and your mind.

Daily Practice: Work on and toward developing faith in God or a higher power, yourself, and those your keep in your inner circle.

Believe in your experience, knowledge, skill, and abilities with an emphasis on improvement.

AUGUST 10

You are the BEST!

Now, make today and every day the best day of your life.

Notwithstanding that challenges happen, results come from your faith in God (higher power), yourself, and the realization and clarity of your desired outcomes.

While it may not seem like it, challenges do make you stronger and build your determination.

AUGUST 11

Every person is tested in one way or another. What is important is not that these challenges arise, but how you choose to deal with them when they do arise.

The lessons that you learn from these experiences are a part of the learning—prerequisites in attaining your goals.

AUGUST 12

_____

The Law of 3 indicates that you should focus on the top 3 productive or "High Leverage Activities" (HLAs) that move you in the direction of your objective or destination.

Develop a laser focus on these three activities.

What are your "Law of 3" top three HLAs?

1.
_____
_____

2.
_____
_____

3.
_____
_____

AUGUST 13

Challenge: Today and every day, do something special and unexpected for someone you don't know, even if it appears that they don't deserve it.

It will make your day and change your perspective—and even your life.

AUGUST 14

───────────────

The only way to prepare for tomorrow is to follow through and complete today those HIGH LEVERAGE ACTIVITIES that you have committed to.

Decide, commit, and execute!

Leave nothing for tomorrow.

AUGUST 15

Every day can be a great day if you so choose.

My answer to the common question "How are you?" is this: "I'm always awesome! Thank you for asking."

From time to time someone will challenge me on this and will usually say, "Seriously, every day? Come on, really, how are things?"

Without question, there are going to be days that present interesting, unwanted, and unexpected challenges, and that's alright. You got this. You already know how to deal with challenges that show up.

I choose how my days go and how awesome they are, and so can you. It is your decision.

AUGUST 16

Opportunities are all around you.

You need to be aware.
You need to be prepared.
You need to be ready to accept.
You need to do what others won't do.
You need to embrace challenges.
You need to execute, no matter what.
You need to work as no one else will.
You need to be ready to experience the results of your input.
You need to act without having all the answers.
You need to put your goal and the anticipated results in writing…. now!

AUGUST 17

The learning experiences that count the most are the ones that come unexpectedly and are usually accompanied by some trials and challenges, whether perceived or real.

Real growth is the direct result of trials, tribulations, and failures. These experiences mold you, teach you, and motivate you to become better and more effective as you execute on your genius.

AUGUST 18

Take every opportunity to contribute something positive toward someone else's life. You just may give them a bigger reason to live and contribute their genius to the world.

It can start with a smile from you. Make a difference and change the outlook or perspective of those who are the recipients of this great shift that is a gift.

You can make the shift… decide to do it today!

AUGUST 19

If you're still breathing, you can do it!

Let nothing stop you, for any reason.

Do more today than you did yesterday! Now, go do that every day.

AUGUST 20

Thank you.

Thank you for being you.
Thank you for your contributions.
Thank you for your interest in learning.
Thank you for adding value to others.
Thank you for those things you do that you don't ever get recognized for.
Thank you for making a difference on this planet.
Thank you for your courage.
Thank you for loving your genius.
Thank you for being strong.
Thank you for being a great friend.
Thank you for being honest.
Thank you for being authentic.
Thank you for sharing your knowledge.
Thank you for your faith.
Thank you for sharing your experiences.
Thank you for doing what others won't do.
Thank you for your encouragement.
Thank you for your trust.
Thank you for sharing your love.

Thank you for being you.

AUGUST 21

What to you may seem insignificant may mean the world to another person. Make it your habit, today and every day, to share something fantastic with another human. You may share:

- A smile
- A handshake
- Your time
- Your money
- Your home
- Your food
- A nod
- Your knowledge
- Your faith
- Your belief in them

You may:

- Hold the door for someone
- Help someone across the street
- Give someone a ride
- Say hello
- Help a neighbor with their yard or sidewalk
- Visit a senior
- Be a big brother or sister
- Go for a walk with a new friend

The list could go on for pages, and you can make your own list. Every act, and every person on this planet, is significant. Now, please go share!

AUGUST 22

Life is so beautiful when you take a moment or two to enjoy it.

Time is precious. Enjoy the small moments in life, relish in them just as you do the bigger experiences.

Understanding and living this way will move you from success to significance. There is a massive difference between the two.

AUGUST 23

———————————

At this very moment, there are opportunities just waiting to be discovered by you.

Embrace opportunities, as they are intended for you, and they give your life meaning and your dreams wings.

Explore and embrace one new opportunity every day.

AUGUST 24

Experiences are the spice of life.

Search for, create, and embrace experiences as you encounter them. They were designed for you. They add to who you are becoming.

AUGUST 25

Exercise your Power Source. Your mind is the last unexplored frontier—continue to stretch and expand it.

You were created (and are) one of the most intelligent beings on this planet.

Thinking is the one thing that separates us from the animal forms of life. Use this to your advantage and use it wisely. It is your biggest and most powerful asset.

AUGUST 26

You already have what it takes.

Your potential. Recognize it, excavate it, and intentionally pull the trigger on what you know you are capable of and can bring to fruition.

Time is your friend when you choose to exploit every single minute that you've been gifted with.

AUGUST 27

One of the biggest differences between high achievers and those who are not is the "Speed of Implementation."

No matter how some may justify it, waiting for something to change or be different will never serve you.

Start right now!

AUGUST 28

Reminder: Step into your fears and embrace them. This is the only way you can grow.

Growth comes from knowing, acknowledging, embracing, and moving into your fears.

Today is the best day of your life!

AUGUST 29

One of your many gifts is your ability to choose to be happy. The world needs you and your gift.

1. Chose to be happy
2. Live happily
3. Share your happiness with the world

AUGUST 30

Every moment is new, and every moment is an opportunity. Consciously choose to embrace every opportunity.

Your future self will thank you.

AUGUST 31

Today is the most important day of your life. Treat it that way.

- ❖ Embrace it.
- ❖ Share it.
- ❖ Work it.
- ❖ Learn from it.
- ❖ Make it your masterpiece.

September

Power

"You were gifted with immense power at birth. Most unconsciously choose not to tap into it.
It's yours, utilize it to achieve more than societal norms allow for."
– Shawn Shewchuk

For the month of September, we talk about power—your power. It has always been yours, gifted to you at birth by your creator. It is incumbent on you to recognize and utilize this incredible, life-changing gift.

SEPTEMBER 1

Clear communication is one of the keys to harnessing your power in the achievement of your goals and objectives.

If there are things that are unclear to you, have the guts to take the initiative and clarify these gray areas today.

SEPTEMBER 2

Pick your opportunities. Every day there is an abundance of opportunities that are yours just for the taking; you just need to ask and be ready to accept.

You will, of course, need to execute.

Pick → Ask → Accept → Execute

SEPTEMBER 3

You know what fear is and what it feels like. You will need to face your fears and you need to be aware of how you change the paradigm of fear. This allows you to move forward and do it consistently.

By facing your fears, you will overcome and power through them.

Take this opportunity to stay in your power place.

SEPTEMBER 4

Your power is realized, and your dreams are fulfilled, when you embrace your biggest fears and execute the activity you've been avoiding. It is your biggest opportunity.

SEPTEMBER 5

You are a genius.

Leave mediocrity behind and light your imagination on fire. Yes, you can!

SEPTEMBER 6

Your decision on how you kickstart your morning determines the outcome of your day.

You have the power to experience the day that you deserve, every day. Exercise that power every morning.

SEPTEMBER 7

What may appear as your darkest day will become your pivot point and produce the greatest gift.

Every day and every experience molds you into the human it was always intended for you to become.

SEPTEMBER 8

The way we treat those around us, no matter their circumstances, determines our own future. View every interaction as an opportunity to make a positive difference in someone's life.

Just so you know, this also positively impacts *your* life. 😊

SEPTEMBER 9

Eliminate your escape routes. Forget about the safety net.

Jump!

Enable yourself to make real, significant, and lasting change by letting go of what is _perceived_ as secure.

SEPTEMBER 10

You have it all. You are perfect just the way you were created.

Use and multiply your gifts to the benefit of all around you.

You deserve a life of abundance.

SEPTEMBER 11

Power move: Gratitude and the Law of 3's.

Make time every day, multiple times throughout the day, to express gratitude for all that you have been blessed with.

It will change your outlook and your day.

What are the first 3 things that come to mind that you are grateful for?

1. _____
   _____

2. _____
   _____

3. _____
   _____

SEPTEMBER 12

Increase your income by doubling whatever you invest in you. Personal and professional development are the difference-makers.

Focus on mastery by beginning to actively invest time, energy, effort, and money in yourself today!

SEPTEMBER 13

Refuse to allow your past to destroy your beautiful future.

Take a moment to paint a picture in words of your beautiful future. Engage with this activity before you move on with anything else.

_____
_____
_____
_____
_____
_____
_____
_____
_____
_____
_____
_____

SEPTEMBER 14

When you figure out your why, the future becomes clear and achievement of what seemed impossible becomes a burning desire. That allows you to accomplish anything you set your mind to.

Set your mind to the possible. Achieve the impossible.

What is your why?

SEPTEMBER 15

It's time to utilize your gifts and create the change that you long for in your life.

What are your gifts, and what is the change you desire in your life?

SEPTEMBER 16

You can do anything you set your mind to, but you just can't do it with the sofa seatbelt on.

Unbuckle and unleash!

SEPTEMBER 17

Life lesson: While important, starting can be rough. Know that there is equality in both the start and the finish.

Start now! Finish strong!

SEPTEMBER 18

With every breath, you are an example to the world. Yes, people are watching life happen and the result of your choices.

Every day, choose to be a beacon of progress, learning, hope, faith, and love. Every individual seeks light; you are that light, if even to just one soul.

Believe!

Shine your light.

SEPTEMBER 19

You are the center of someone's universe. Even if you are unaware of it, someone is watching your every step.

Be proud of the path you have chosen; someone is following in your footsteps.

SEPTEMBER 20

Opportunities avail themselves to those who dedicate the required effort and energy to move up the ladder a few rungs to the extraordinary.

Exploit your extraordinary!

SEPTEMBER 21

Leave the garbage in the garbage.

Choose to consciously focus on the good and permit only those thoughts that expand, elevate, and lead to execution and improved results.

SEPTEMBER 22

_____

Practice growing and stretching your boundaries. Challenge yourself to go BIG!

Law of 3's: Outline your top three "Big Picture" objectives below.

1. _____
   _____

2. _____
   _____

3. _____
   _____

Now double those goals.

SEPTEMBER 23

―――――――――

The most precious gift you can give anyone is your time.

Cherish it. Treasure it.

It isn't free.

SEPTEMBER 24

Just because you can't quite make out the finish line doesn't mean you shouldn't start.

Most people stop before they even start. Start strong, finish even stronger.

SEPTEMBER 25

Let go of self-criticism and move forward; overcome by using the knowledge gained from challenges.

Your confidence in you, your knowledge, and your abilities will make the difference between where you are and where you want to be.

SEPTEMBER 26

Believe in yourself.

Have the confidence that you can overcome the obstacles that may come your way.

Believe that you can achieve great things while learning from the obstacles that you may face as you journey toward your destination.

SEPTEMBER 27

You have the answer!

You are the answer!

No one is going to save you. You have full control of your life.

Now that you've been reminded of that, take 100% responsibility for your life at this very moment.

SEPTEMBER 28

Time is a gift.

It's how you choose to utilize your gift that makes the difference between mediocrity and significance and, to a lesser degree, success.

SEPTEMBER 29

Communicate, engage, converse, resolve, and become solution-centric.

No matter how you may feel or what your viewpoint is at this very moment, there is ALWAYS a solution.

Learn from the situation or problem but don't focus on it. Place a concerted focus only on lessons learned and solutions.

SEPTEMBER 30

Inspiration comes from your wants, not from your needs.

You already know how to attract into your life what you need. It is easy.

Place a focus on and invest your energy into what it is you genuinely want.

This creates drive and enthusiasm; momentum and results.

October

Life

"You were created for a reason. You were gifted this life for a reason. You woke up this morning for a reason. You serve others in your own way for a reason. You are reading this for a reason.

Your life is invaluable. You are the highest form of creation. You are not here by chance."
– Shawn Shewchuk

For the month of October, we look at life—your life. Why you were born and why you exist.
The reason that you woke up this morning and
the impact you have having.
And get ready for it—you aren't here by chance.

OCTOBER 1

Thank you for being you. You are a blessing.

Be grateful for every twist and turn. Embrace every experience no matter how you perceive it. Your outlook determines your outcome from every experience.

Be grateful for everyone whether they're in your life or not. You may see them every day or you haven't seen them in decades—express gratitude.

OCTOBER 2

Believe me when I tell you that everyone has a unique purpose in life and extraordinary talent to give and share with others.

Be a blessing to other people. Make a commitment to serve others.

Serving your fellow humans is the best thing you can do to make a difference.

OCTOBER 3

There is no rehearsal in life. Start living life on your terms, as if tomorrow doesn't exist.

If you are unsure of something, get clarity before deciding, and then do it quickly. Clarify your purpose and clarify your goals. Clarify your why.

Opportunities and life wait for no one.

Awareness and clarity go hand in hand and will empower you to avoid the crippling paralysis by analysis trap.

Today isn't a test drive, it's the real deal. Make it count!

OCTOBER 4

If you want to achieve positive results, you need to cultivate a positive attitude. Your attitude toward other people and all forms of life determines how they will respond or react toward you. Your attitude is the determinant of ALL your outcomes.

Always maintain a positive and joyful attitude, and you will experience the corresponding results.

Question: What do you do to ensure that you have a positive attitude?

Answer: Ensure that the three components of your attitude – your thoughts, your feelings, and your actions – are all aligned. Of course, this is also based on the ideal I mentioned above about your Positive Attitude.

OCTOBER 5

Everything starts with awareness and expands as you make conscious choices.

Your choices are THE determinant of the level of success in life that you ultimately achieve.

As there are no guarantees, how do you know if you are making the right decisions?

Live in the moment and make decisions for your future. Make every effort to be aware of not just what you want as an outcome today, but also of the future impact and outcomes that will manifest as a result of your decision today.

OCTOBER 6

Only pre-determined action steps will move you in the direction of your objectives and goals.

Reverse engineer your goals to develop a plan, then outline your action steps. This will empower you to successfully reach your destination.

What are you waiting for?

If you have already decided what to do, how to do it, and where to go—act fast!

Write down 3 High Leverage Activities (HLAs) you will execute and accomplish today and that will move you toward your goals and objectives:

1._____
_____

2._____
_____

3._____
_____

OCTOBER 7

Your thoughts become things. Your internal conversations are all-powerful. Your life is an open book.

Your conversations with others have an impact, even if you may not be aware of what that is.

Offer your support, hope, motivation, and words of encouragement, and always approach a conversation from the point of view of service.

OCTOBER 8

Be on guard. Refuse to allow the unwanted words and actions of others to influence you. Be critical about what you allow in. Your outcomes and level of achievement are a direct reflection of what you decide is important to you.

When you decide that your results are important to you, decide first to refuse the opinions and detracting comments from others.

OCTOBER 9

───────────

How do you utilize your time during the day? Are you spending time with family and friends? Helping your neighbors?

Are you investing your only non-renewable resource in productive activities that ensure outcomes that you need, want, desire, and ultimately deserve?

Plan out what activities you are going to do during a specific timeframe. Make sure that when you invest time, the activities you engage in are moving you in the direction of your goals and objectives.

Time is without a question our greatest non-renewable resource.

OCTOBER 10

Just as we were not meant to live in poverty, we were also not meant to live without challenges. Achievements would not be as rewarding if we didn't encounter obstacles and have to overcome them on our way there.

Challenges are the experiences that change and mold you – your perspectives – and give you the impetus to seek other paths and higher levels of awareness.

Determining an alternative path may mean seeking new opportunities, hiring a coach, and choosing a new group of like-minded (Mastermind) humans.

OCTOBER 11

Once you know what you want, you have to know what it's worth to you.

A clear understanding of what motivates you – the size of your WHY – is key to both collapsing time frames and achieving your goals in less time.

Two questions for you:

What is your why?
_____
_____
_____
_____
_____

How big is your why?
_____
_____
_____
_____
_____

OCTOBER 12

You can spearhead change right from where you are today. Don't wait for something to change or someone else to do something.

Live your life on your terms, with a clear focus on what is important to you and those you love.

OCTOBER 13

You will encounter obstacles anytime you decide to implement change.

This is how we learn and grow. Just as there are life lessons as we mature chronologically, this too takes place in our mindset and growth in knowledge and awareness.

Seek to learn. Become a sponge.

Invest your time, energy, effort, and money to continue growing and to become the individual and example that it was always intended that you become.

OCTOBER 14

———————————

1. Start.
2. Goal.
3. Plan.
4. Misstep.
5. Execute.
6. Experience.
7. Share.
8. Repeat.

Waiting will not get you to where you want to be.

OCTOBER 15

Most extraordinarily successful people were not born with silver spoons in their mouths.

They set massive growth-oriented goals and worked toward them fearlessly and relentlessly.

My commitment:

☐ I unreservedly commit to pursuing my goals relentlessly, without regard for detractors or other real or perceived stumbling blocks.

☐ I refuse to permit fear in any of its forms to impede my progress in the achievement of my goals.

☐ I promise to be true to myself as I pursue my dreams and goals while making a conscious contribution to those with whom I come into contact.

OCTOBER 16

We don't place enough value on time until we are faced with how little we have.

Treasure and leverage every moment.

Boredom and the idea of "killing time" are for those who don't have a dream or want more than misery or a status-quo life.

OCTOBER 17

Those who are hugely successful are not focused solely on themselves but rather on what they can do for others and how they can serve.

How are you serving others today?

OCTOBER 18

Accountability, innovation, and execution are prerequisites for achieving any goal you've set for yourself.

Decide how to apply these three imperatives today.

OCTOBER 19

The most successful people in history have an unwavering belief in themselves and extreme faith in the source, higher power, or God.

How strong are your beliefs and faith? Get clear on the strength of your beliefs and your level of faith. Detail it below.

Belief in Self:

_____
_____
_____
_____
_____
_____

Faith in the Source, Higher Power, or God:

_____
_____
_____
_____
_____
_____

OCTOBER 20

You receive 86,400 gifts a day. These gifts are the most incredible and valuable gifts you will ever receive. Every one of those 86,400 seconds is extremely valuable, and you get to experience each just one time.

Every moment is a gift. Refuse the temptation to squander your gifts. LIVE, LEARN, LOVE, and LEVERAGE those moments. When you examine life closely, that is all you have.

OCTOBER 21

Life is about only three things. Those three things are as follows, and these apply to everyone, including you and those you care about.

1. Life is about people and the relationships you have with those people.

2. Life is about freedom—you living your life with the freedom that you have designed.

3. Life is about you fulfilling your destiny—living, giving, and contributing to this world the way you were intended to.

OCTOBER 22
_____

Open your mind and allow yourself to dream in order to find what you really want out of your life.

Dreamers are the builders. Dream and be a builder.

OCTOBER 23

The small things are the most important. Those ongoing, small victories will become a tidal wave of success.

You need to:

Be a <u>Starter</u>   Get moving on your own immediately.

Gain <u>Clarity</u>   Get crystal clear on your destination.

Be <u>Tenacious</u>   Never give up, no matter what barriers may appear.

Become Laser-<u>Focused</u>   To the exclusion of all outside distractions.

<u>Execute</u>   On pre-determined action steps. Act!

Possess <u>Determination</u>   Know what you deserve and go after it with everything you have.

OCTOBER 24

Conformity kills creativity.

Think about it. If you're doing it because everyone else is doing it, stop! Everyone else doesn't want the results and the outcomes that you want and are actively pursuing.

You are unique. You are a part of that small minority that knows there is more, is determined to attain that goal, and will do anything that is needed to achieve that objective, provided it's legal, moral, and ethical.

OCTOBER 25

You have to be ready for change and want it badly enough to pursue it. Be ready for what you are seeking.

Be ready for and accept success.

The drivers of change:

____ Your Why
____ Your Goal
____ Your Wants
____ Your Love
____ Your Dreams
____ Your Motivation
____ Your Inspiration
____ Your Acceptance
____ Your Results

OCTOBER 26

Your attitude comprises three components.

1. Thoughts
2. Feelings
3. Actions

To change your results, you must first change and align your thoughts, feelings, and actions.

A great attitude is the driver of improved results and strong, powerful, and high-trust relationships.

OCTOBER 27

You must grasp the fact that your past does not equal your future, and let it go.

You've learned from the past. You've experienced the past. You've succeeded and failed in the past.

Don't live in the past.

Utilize and leverage your knowledge and experiences gained in the past to augment your future.

Your past doesn't have to define you.

OCTOBER 28

Recap: Invest in your personal growth.

To succeed in your own personal growth you will have to dedicate time, expend effort, devote energy, and invest money.

This is the only way that you can truly succeed in the ongoing growth that will last your entire life and deliver what you seek and deserve.

OCTOBER 29

Don't let your roadblocks stop you from going where you want to go.

Don't allow negative thoughts to dominate your thinking.

Instead, rethink your plans. If you feel overwhelmed, stop and break the situation into smaller pieces, then strategically tackle one piece at a time.

Just don't let the roadblock stop you from pushing forward. Whether you step over, go around, or create a new path, there will always be a way to overcome your roadblocks and turn them into steppingstones.

OCTOBER 30

Resist the temptation to step back into the old habits. This is the easy path and will not lead you to achieve what you deserve.

Pursue greatness. Expect and receive the gifts as they are presented. Power through all the other distractions.

OCTOBER 31

Who do you want to be five or ten years from now?

Decide who you want to be. You can then determine where you want to focus your time and resources.

Remember that only you have the power to create your own destiny.

You are powerful!

November

Speed of Implementation

*"The first step is the most crucial. Without the
first step, nothing happens.
The time for the first step is today. Tomorrow is not
guaranteed."
— Shawn Shewchuk*

For the month of November, we examine why some of us get there faster than others and why some never make it at all. Those who succeed, and collapse timeframes while doing it, act without hesitation. These action steps are not taken just for the sake of acting—they are bite-sized pieces of the Big Hairy Audacious Goal. They are pre-determined but not labored over and dissected until unrecognizable. Paralysis by analysis is not a component of leveling up your results.

You have to initiate the process today. You must take real, quantified, and predetermined action steps that you have arrived at based on the reverse engineering of your goal. You need the bite-sized pieces.

NOVEMBER 1

Give thanks always!

Take a moment every day; be grateful for the small things as well as the large.

Be thankful for those thought-provoking individuals and possible challenges. Without them, you wouldn't be the incredible human that you've become.

Express gratitude at every opportunity.

Take every opportunity to share your gratitude with every individual with whom you come into contact, and beyond. Being thankful leads to happiness, and that is contagious.

NOVEMBER 2

Believe in yourself.

It is essential to your success.

Trusting in your competence will attract to you a positive response. Whether it is in your life, business, or career, believing in yourself is one of the first steps toward success.

NOVEMBER 3

Your thoughts create your life. Yesterday's thoughts created today's, and today's thoughts create tomorrow's.

What you are creating every minute of every day?

Start right now!

Start creating the life you desire and deserve.

NOVEMBER 4

There is always an opportunity. It is up to you to find it.

Every day is a new opportunity for you.

Each day gives you the opportunity to be grateful. To learn. To live. To love. To grow and be a better version of yourself.

NOVEMBER 5

Believe in your ideas and dare to imagine the next milestone.

Set milestones on your journey that are motivating and, upon reaching them, celebrate your successes. Your successes are huge motivators.

NOVEMBER 6
_____

It's time to utilize your gifts and create the change in your life that you have been yearning for.

NOVEMBER 7

Each day is a gift and an opportunity to make a positive difference.

NOVEMBER 8
_____

There are no limits on what you can accomplish, other than the ones you impose.

NOVEMBER 9
_____

Failure is not defeat. You are only defeated when you do not persist.

NOVEMBER 10
_____

It's the small things in life that are important. Don't take them for granted.

NOVEMBER 11

Give humble thought and immense gratitude for those who came before and gave the ultimate sacrifice so that you would have the opportunities that freedom affords you.

Take just a few moments today and express your gratitude to one of the heroes that put their lives on the line, or who gave their lives so that you could live the life that you have.

Some gave it all!

If you are one of those that is or was willing to give it all in service and put it all out there… Thank you. Thank you.

NOVEMBER 12

Take control of your own situation. Put yourself on the road to prosperity.

Each morning you wake up is a battle and a challenge whether you like it or not. It doesn't have to be that way. It's time to take control of your own life and face it head-on. You can choose to just sit back and watch your life pass by or you can choose to take control of your life and be the champion of it.

Which one will you choose?

NOVEMBER 13
_____

Always be grateful for the gift of time and beware of its fragility and fleetingness.

NOVEMBER 14

Always give, even when you don't need to and especially when you're not required to.

The true sign of a selfless human is the ability to give unreservedly, with a sole focus on the benefits to the recipient.

NOVEMBER 15

Problems are really opportunities waiting to be exposed and leveraged.

NOVEMBER 16
_____

Stop doing the things that are unproductive and incongruent with your goals and objectives.

NOVEMBER 17

Just because you failed doesn't mean you were defeated.

Temporary defeat doesn't make you a failure.

Don't be deceived or discouraged by defeat. Know that there is hope.

Dust it off. Learn from it and ask yourself "What did I learn from this experience?"

Then go at it again—only this time you aren't going to try. You are going punch right through your goal.

NOVEMBER 18
_____

Whatever we concentrate on will manifest into reality.

NOVEMBER 19

Your thoughts today are a good indicator of your results tomorrow.

What is your tomorrow going to bring?

Only you can determine how big a success tomorrow will be for you.

NOVEMBER 20

Surround yourself with phenomenal people. Grow with like-minded people and be of service to all people.

Make this your mantra and work on it daily.

NOVEMBER 21

Start now; don't wait until you or the situation or something else is perfect. "It" will never be perfect.

Nothing, including tomorrow, is promised; this includes what you may think you could have accomplished.

All you have is this moment.

NOVEMBER 22

Ready, set, go...

You are only running a race against yourself. Decide you are the winner.

And the winner is?

NOVEMBER 23

Engage with, invest time with, and mastermind with like-minded and motivated people daily.

The results will astound you.

NOVEMBER 24

Commitment leads to accomplishment in all areas of your life.

Be proud of your accomplishments and celebrate them regularly.

NOVEMBER 25

Your purpose is defined by you and is the secret to your results.

Your entire life, and what you achieve in life, is predicated upon the decisions you make and the goals you commit to.

Even if you are unaware of it, there is always a higher power at work in your life and your world. This higher power will deliver whatever you focus on and ask of it.

What are you focused on? What are you asking for?

NOVEMBER 26

Look up, not down. Look ahead, not behind. And seek fulfillment.

NOVEMBER 27

Your gifts are unique to you and are unlike anyone else's.

NOVEMBER 28

If you look hard enough, you will find reasons why you should have a false start. Stop looking for why you shouldn't. Passionately find reasons why you should move forward, and then do it without hesitation.

Hesitation increases risk and empowers you to fail.

NOVEMBER 29

Stand for something worthwhile, something that will make you and those you love proud.

NOVEMBER 30
_____

You are ready to go!

You know what to do. You know when to do it. You know how to do it. You know why you have to do it.

Start this instant!

December

The Difference

"You are the difference. You make the difference. You are the difference-maker.
– Shawn Shewchuk

For the month of December, we delve into "The Difference" and how you have already made the decision to be different and create a difference. Trust me when I tell you that it's a good thing; you want to stand out and experience the difference that being different makes. Somewhere around 98% of the world is the same, indifferent, beige—but you are not. You are special, unique, and different, all because you decided to be different, to make a difference, and to create a different outcome for you and those you love.

DECEMBER 1

Expand your thoughts and beliefs. You are about to embark on one of the greatest odysseys of your life.

You are about to take another trip around the sun. Make this journey one for the record books.

Take some special time today and outline below what your life will look like on December 31st next year.

Go BIG!

12 months from now my life will be...

_____
_____
_____
_____
_____
_____
_____
_____
_____
_____

DECEMBER 2

Embrace your power; become engaged with your life.

Your level of engagement determines your outcomes.

Become emotionally engaged with your goals and your results. Watch the dramatic change that you want and deserve unfolding before your eyes.

DECEMBER 3
_____

Conduct yourself in a manner that you never have in the past and take massive action.

If not now, when?

You can't count on tomorrow.

DECEMBER 4

We were all created equal; however, some of us decide to accomplish more in less time and leave a lasting impact.

What are you accomplishing, and what is your timeframe?

Get clear on this by writing it out below.

What you are accomplishing?

_____
_____
_____
_____
_____
_____
_____

In what timeframe?

_____
_____
_____
_____
_____
_____
_____

DECEMBER 5

You will undoubtedly face challenges (perceived or real), and either way, the only important thing for you to understand is how you deal with them when they do show up.

YOU ARE IN CONTROL!

DECEMBER 6

Once you know where you are going, life becomes simpler.

Where are you going?

DECEMBER 7

The world needs more open-minded people.

Always approach everything you do from multiple perspectives.

DECEMBER 8

When on their deathbed, no one wishes they had spent more time working or regrets not having acquired more materialistic things.

Find, embrace, and expend energy on what you are passionate about; what is making a difference.

DECEMBER 9

Setting big goals will force you to quickly attain the necessary resources.

Go big and start learning immediately. It'll pay off with life-altering rewards.

DECEMBER 10

Fear does not exist outside of your mind.

Banish the conditioning and self-imposed limitations that fear creates.

You can do anything that you set your mind to!

DECEMBER 11

Let go of those misplaced ideals and experiences that are restricting you and inhibiting your progress.

Holding on will not serve you. Anything that won't serve you – that you attempt to hold on to or suppress – will poison you, your relationships, and your desired outcomes.

Positive forward movement is achieved through release, a reframe, a refocus, and ultimately in doing something dramatically different… otherwise known as change.

DECEMBER 12

More of the same gives you more of the same.

Rethink how you view and approach every aspect of your life and then redefine your execution, based on the outcomes you want to experience in your life.

Refuse to accept anything other than what will get you to where you want to be.

Our world needs more visionaries.

DECEMBER 13

_____

Daily Practice: Develop a habit of growing and stretching your boundaries, challenging yourself to attain larger objectives.

DECEMBER 14

Real and lasting results come from realizing your dreams – through raw determination and effort – while focused on the predetermined execution steps developed when you set your destination.

Start executing!

Daily Practice: Develop faith in yourself and your abilities.

DECEMBER 15

Our world needs you to step up and be the you that God, the source, or higher power intended you to be.

DECEMBER 16

Opportunities avail themselves to those who dedicate the required change; to go up the ladder a few rungs to the extraordinary.

Determine your level of extraordinary at this very moment.

DECEMBER 17

It's your time to join the 2%.

Somewhere around 98% of people today are merely subsisting and striving to "make it." Most don't even know what that means.

This isn't all about money. It is about fulfillment and significance. While money is important in our society, money is a byproduct of the level of service we deliver when we show up.

You are already on your way!

DECEMBER 18

Winning is accomplished through planning, dedication, creativity, activity management, execution, incredible experiences, and the most important one of all—people.

You were born a winner. It's yours for the taking.

DECEMBER 19

Wishing and hoping is not the path to fulfillment and success.

Predetermined actions and execution lead us in the right direction.

Stop wishing and start doing.

DECEMBER 20

Recap: If you already know how to do it, it's not a goal. The sole purpose of goals is growth.

Commit to something so big that it scares you.

Stretch yourself!

Grow!

DECEMBER 21

Stand for something that will leave a trail long after you're gone... your legacy.

DECEMBER 22

Develop the ability to think for yourself.

Most people today are surviving based on the negative trash they have internalized. Your first goal is to be different.

Refuse to ride the next cloud. Instead, use your highest faculties to build the life that was always intended for you.

Thrive!

DECEMBER 23

There are people who take responsibility for where they are in their lives and those who shirk responsibility by blaming other people or circumstances for their own lack of action.

Live your dreams by living the life you've determined you want to live. Living any other way is living someone else's life.

Live YOUR life every day!

DECEMBER 24

As the new year rapidly approaches, take time today to reflect on what has transpired in your life and your initiatives since we started this daily journey together.

Open your heart and mind to how you can give, serve, and support others, not just at this time of year but all year long.

DECEMBER 25

Today is a day of celebration.

Celebration is about what is important to you.

Celebrate your family, your faith, your accomplishments, and all things good. The best time investment that you can make today is time with those you care for and love, and time to celebrate.

It's your life. If you want to up-level your celebration, go find someone or more than one person to celebrate with. Today is about people, created just as you were.

Merry Christmas and Happy Holidays.

DECEMBER 26

Life isn't about things. While things are important, they are not the core of your journey. Create a life built around experiences with those you care for and love.

This is not a given; it takes determination, effort, focus, and understanding.

This year has been the beginning of your redefined legacy.

DECEMBER 27

Your choices impact you, your family, and those around you. Your choices determine your results, both today and in the future.

Get crystal clear on what your future will look like because you have the paintbrush. You are the artist that ultimately determines what the picture portrays.

DECEMBER 28

When given a choice, take the more difficult path. While initially it may appear impossible, the reward that you will receive upon arrival at your destination is utterly indescribable. The English language fails us in that there are no words sufficient for articulating a description accurate enough in its magnificence.

Your trials and tribulations are all more than worthwhile.

DECEMBER 29

Unwavering commitment is key to your overall and long-term, improved results. Make an irrevocable decision and commitment to fulfill your dreams by executing on your Big Hairy Audacious Goals.

Outline your commitment to yourself to live your dreams.

_____

_____

_____

_____

_____

_____

_____

_____

_____

_____

Now go out and make all your dreams a reality. You have been gifted with the skill of self-leadership and the power to create. Take these incredible talents and work daily to multiply them.

DECEMBER 30

You can climb the tallest mountain, but you must be willing to take the first small step.

Separate yourself from the masses; take one step at a time even when you are unable to see the finish line.

Make the changes necessary to put yourself into the wonderful place where very few go—the top 1%.

DECEMBER 31

Set aside and invest two hours of your time today. This investment will pay massive dividends over the next 12 months and beyond.

The first hour is an Accountability Checkpoint (ACP) for this year. Where are you today in relation to where you were on January 1st of this year?

In the second hour, you will outline in detail where you want to be on December 31st next year. Be extremely clear and specific on what you will accomplish over the next 12 months.

Remember, what you are going to accomplish – the level of impact that you will have – isn't in any way related to what you have done so far in your life.

It's a NEW start!

Where you started this year and where you are in relation to your goal for this year:

Detail as much as you can about where you are going to be a year from today, what you are going to accomplish every month, and the level of impact you are going to have.

January:
_____
_____
_____

February:
_____
_____
_____

March:
_____
_____
_____

April:
_____
_____
_____

May:
_____
_____
_____

June:
_____
_____
_____

July:
_____
_____
_____

August:
_____
_____
_____

September:
_____
_____
_____

October:
_____
_____
_____

November:
_____
_____
_____

December:
_____
_____
_____